Getti...

by...

Consultant:
Adria F. Klein, Ph.D.
California State University, San Bernardino

capstone
classroom

Heinemann Raintree • Red Brick Learning
division of Capstone

People get from here to there in many ways.

People use hot air balloons to move in the air.

People use airplanes to travel across the sky.

People use space shuttles to fly very high.

People use sailboats to travel on water.

People use dogsleds to travel on snow.

Some people travel in cars.

Some people travel by bus.

Some people ride horses on trails.

Some people ride bikes on trails.

Some people travel on a streetcar.

Some people travel in a taxi.

People in this city ride in boats.

People in this city ride on trains.

Some people even use elephants to travel!